Music Minus One Trumpet
Also suitable for any B♭ Instrument

Signature
Series

VOLUME 2

6854

Back to **The Very Thought Of You** and some thoughts on how to approach it. You'll notice that I "hug" the melody throughout and I use the word deliberately because I have so much affection for melody that I really felt no need to stray far from it other than some embellishments and phrasing modifications. Oh yes, I popped the Harmon mute in and played a couple of obbligatos behind the strings before opening up and playing it out until the final "My Love" on high B to G. So, let's call track one a "template" of how to proceed through the remaining seven songs with some exceptions or additions that I'll talk about later.

Harold Arlen's **That Old Black Magic** has been done at various tempos and with brassy, rhythmically complex backgrounds but I chose in the spirit of this album to go with a more traditional version and one that's probably closer to what Mr. Arlen had in mind. Notice the subtle "twists" in his melody in order to provide contrast to the repeated notes and rhythm. This device is a hall-mark of all great composers. In other words, a surprise phrase amidst the expected repetition. The very best example I can recall in classical repertoire is in Mozart's Symphony #40. If you're a Mozart fan as I am, you'll take a listen and I promise you there's much food for thought to apply to jazz improvisation in Wolfgang's creations!

Tenderly, a Sarah Vaughn hit in 1946 and Rosemary Clooney's theme song on her TV variety show is a song that's dear to my heart for it was one of my first trumpet solos. I played it in junior high school with my mother accompanying me on the piano in it's original key of Eb concert and as a waltz.

Notice that I took a bit more liberty with this one, while never intending to re-write such a gorgeous melody. This is the way I suggest approaching this song: It goes through three keys, starting in Bb with the interlude in G and abruptly modulates to A for the "out-chorus". When the ensemble enters, it's your chance to "shine" with some fills that lead back to the melody out. The ob-bligato at the end is what puts a capper on this chart and which makes a statement that it's a trumpet feature piece. By the way, if you want to hear a really brilliant trumpet recording of Tenderly, check out Randy Brooks, who was one of my idols as a young-ster.

Johnny Mathis recorded Errol Garner's **Misty** and made a huge hit out of it in his 1959 album Heavenly and I have fond memories of backing him in the 1960s with a string of concerts in which he inevitably was asked to sing Misty. Note that this is the only track with a click count-off plus your starting note of Bb.

A change of pace with a swinging version of Rosie Clooney's **Hey There.** Rosie rose to fame with the general public as an actress and a singer of novelty songs like Mambo Italiano but she was truly a gifted jazz singer. I had the pleasure of working with her at the Waldorf-Astoria in Manhattan and it was a blast! If you follow the transcription of my solo in the book you'll see and hear that for the first chorus I did a jazzy interpretation of the melody mostly by modifying the rhythms. With the modulation to C, and a really nice, relaxed walking bass line with no piano or as we used to call it "strollin", here's an opportunity to use your Harmon mute while allowing "space" which is of course, silence. Now, I don't mean lengthy silences but rather letting the music "breathe". The two greatest examples of this way of playing in the Harmon are Harry "Sweets" Edison and my idol Miles Davis! You and I can always learn from those two giants! Although, it's rare for the Harmon to be "soaring" above a full big band ensemble, I chose to give'er a go and even end on the high C in the mute rather than suddenly going open. Couldn't leave it at that, so I put a capper on this one too!

Perry Como's **Prisoner Of Love** became a #1 hit in 1946. Also, it's probably right up there as what I call the best "victim" songs with Billie Holiday's My Man deserving top billing in that category. But this lush arrangement transforms what was a simple pop tune of 1931 into something of great expressive potential. If you've had the misfortune of experiencing unrequited love (and who hasn't to some degree) then here's your opportunity to pour your heart out through your horn! A rather unusual modulation occurs after the rubato bridge leading to the last statement of "imprisonment" which is milked at the last note by a really beautiful passage of surprising chord progressions.

Now, talk about a total change of pace, the unique song **Love Dance** is one of my favorites and although written by the supremely gifted Grammy award winning Brazilian musician Ivan Lins, it has more of a contemporary flavor than a Latin one. This 1989 song has the distinction of being one of the most re-recorded songs in history and Carmen McRae's version is delivered with her usual elegance and sophistication. Check her singing it "live" on YouTube. I play and sing this poignant song on live gigs in Naples with Stu Shelton a very talented jazz pianist and I decided to offer it here as a total contrast to the rest of volume two. For lack of a better description, I'll call it a hybrid Jazz Funk Bossa Nova.

Stu came up with a great arrangement that I feel could well be the theme of a Signature Series Volume 3, namely songs associated with contemporary singers and musicians like Sting, Billy Joel and Herbie Hancock. It would be a collection of the best of the new crop of artists and done in a Jazz Funk, Fusion and even what some might call Smooth Jazz genre. Let MMO or me know if this is of interest to you and we'll make it happen with the goal of creating a very special Music Minus One that has high artistic value yet is a practical learning tool.

To end off this volume I've chosen a song by a woman who deserves the title of a musician's singer mainly because she was a fine jazz pianist as well as an extraordinary jazz singer! In the late 1950s while in the USAF stationed in Washington, D.C. with the Air-men of Note, I had the immense honor of not only meeting Shirley Horn but actually sitting in with her one night in the nightclub where she was appearing. Besides being a tremendous talent, she was a most gracious lady with an attitude to match! Ms. Horn's message in her 1992 recording of **Here's To Life** sums up what I would always hope to keep at the forefront of my mind as I go through life with its inevitable ups and downs. It became her signature song and I'm proud to offer my flugel horn rendition here with, I hope, some of the philosophical significance radiating through the musical sounds despite the lack of words.

As with the other songs in this album, I first sang and even recorded vocally prior to the instrumental version in order to deeply implant the story in my mind.

I suggest that you, at the very least, read the lyrics several times to this and the other songs. You will be rewarded, I promise!

Please feel free to email me with questions or feedback from this or any of my other MMOs at bobzottola@naplesjazzlovers.com or visit my website www.naplesjazzlovers.com

All the best!
Bob Zottola
Naples, Florida June 8, 2014

Signature Series

CONTENTS

©2014 MMO Music Group, Inc. All rights reserved.
ISBN 978-1-941566-11-4

MMO 6854

4

SOLO B♭ TRUMPET

The Very Thought Of You

Ray Noble

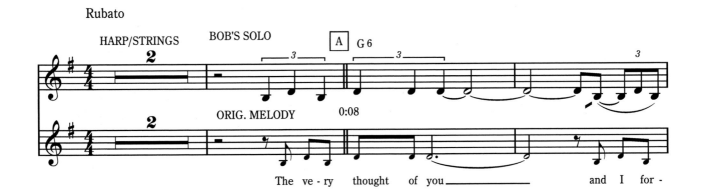

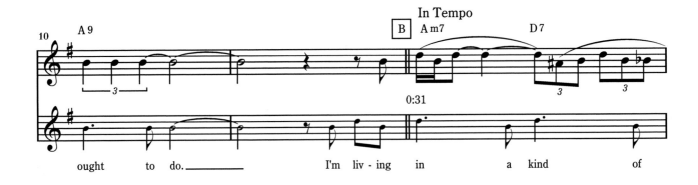

5

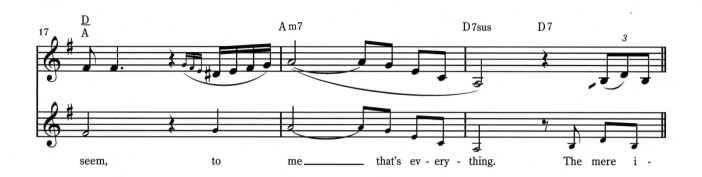

seem, to me_____ that's ev - ery - thing. The mere i -

dea of you,_____ the long - ing here for you,_____ you'll nev - er

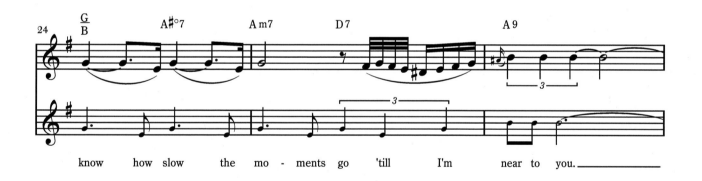

know how slow the mo - ments go 'till I'm near to you._____

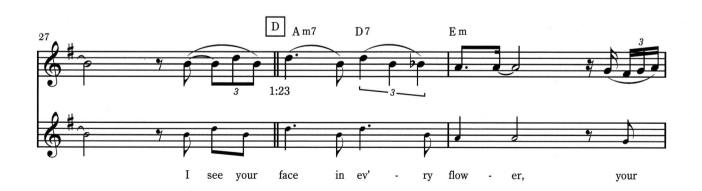

I see your face in ev' - ry flow - er, your

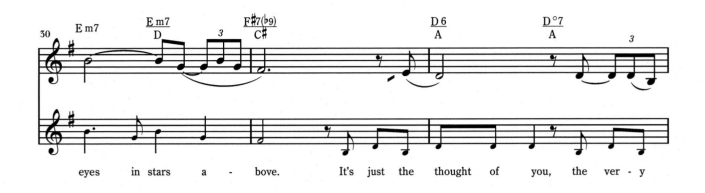

eyes in stars a - bove. It's just the thought of you, the ver - y

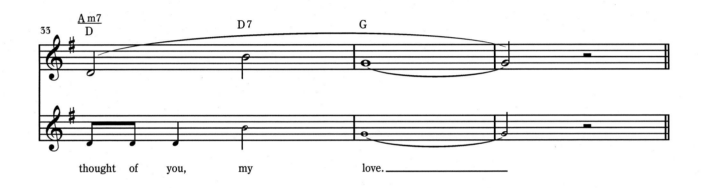

thought of you, my love._____

1:48

2:14

2:39

SOLO B♭ TRUMPET

That Old Black Magic

Harold Arlen

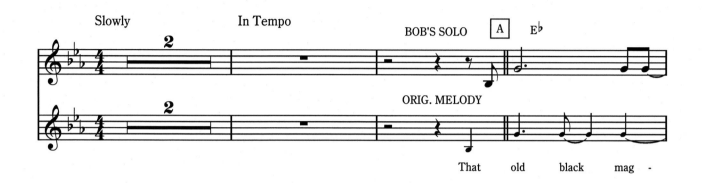

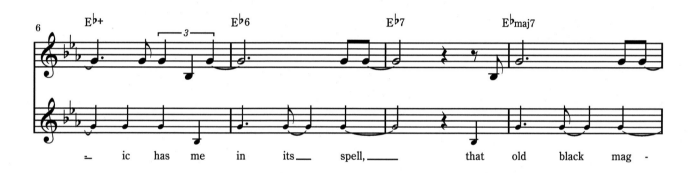

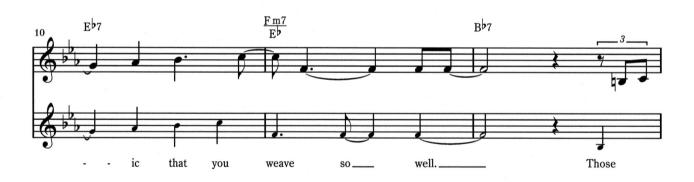

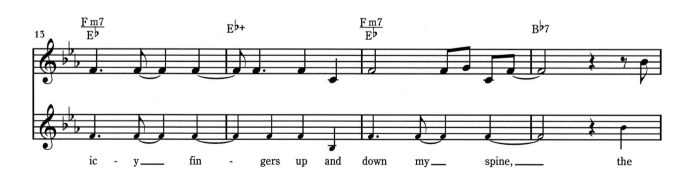

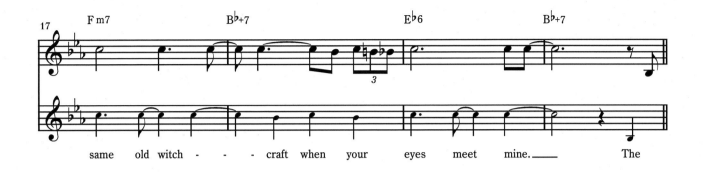

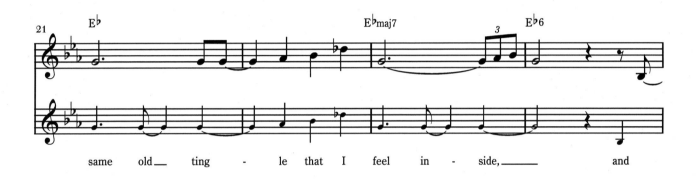

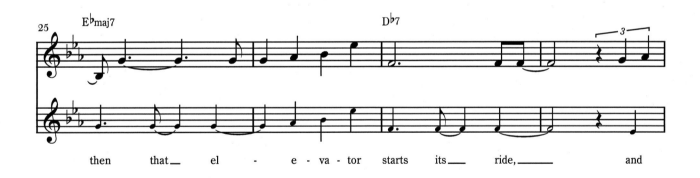

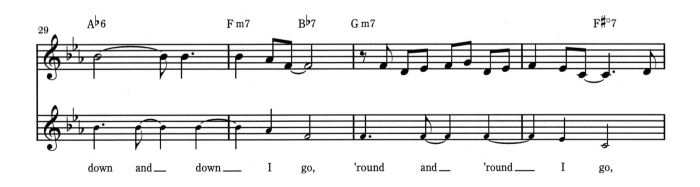

10

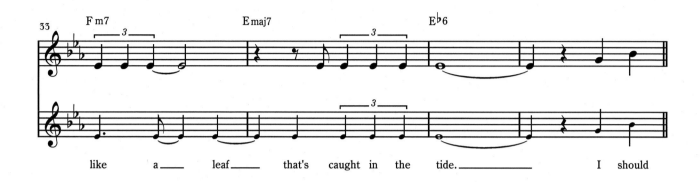

like a ____ leaf ____ that's caught in the tide. _____ I should

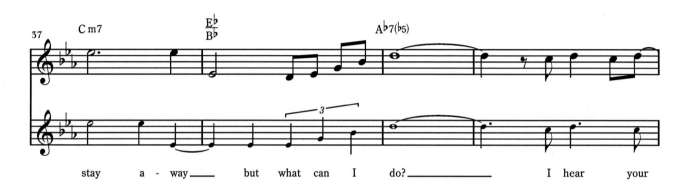

stay a - way ____ but what can I do? _____ I hear your

name _____ and I'm a flame, _____ a

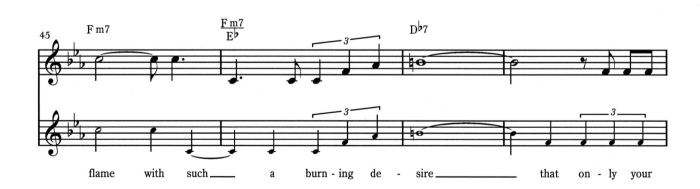

flame with such ____ a burn - ing de - sire _____ that on - ly your

kiss_____ can put out the fire._____ For

you're the __ lov - er I have wait - ed __ for, _____ the

mate that fate_____ had me cre - a - ted for, _____ and

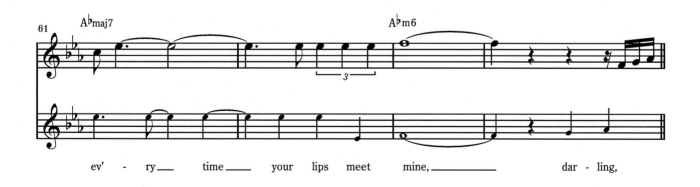

ev' - ry __ time __ your lips meet mine, _____ dar - ling,

12

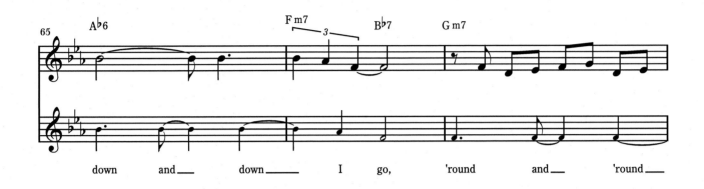

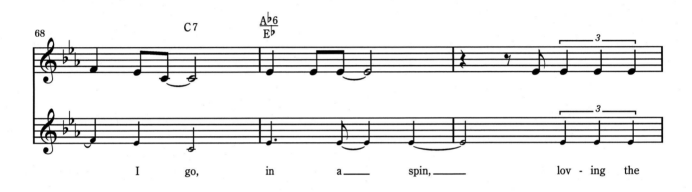

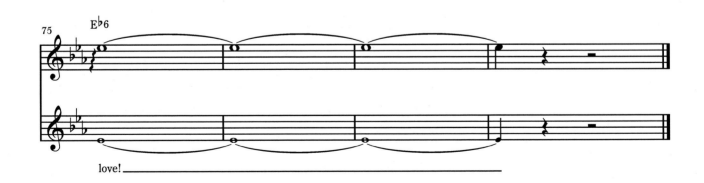

SOLO B♭ TRUMPET

Tenderly

Walter Gross and Jack Lawrence

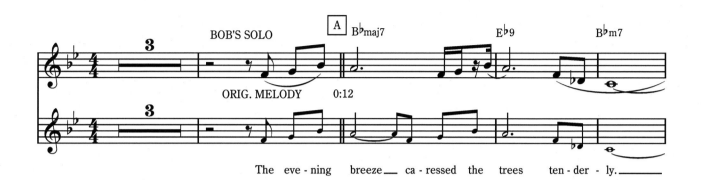

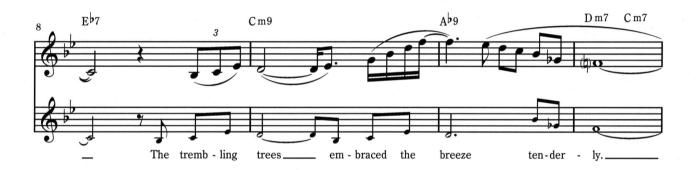

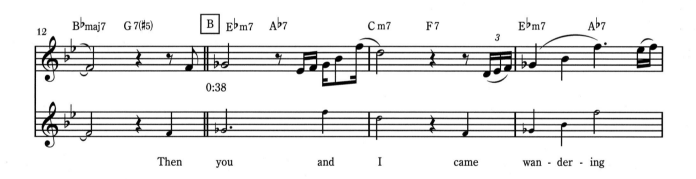

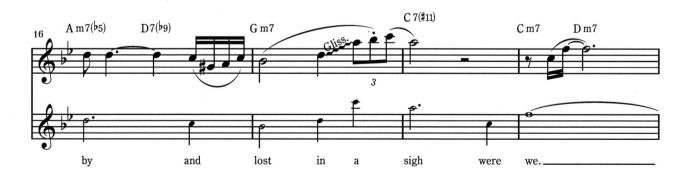

MMO 6854

14

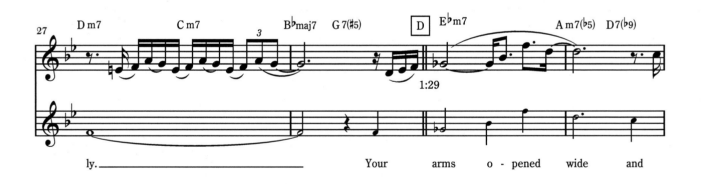

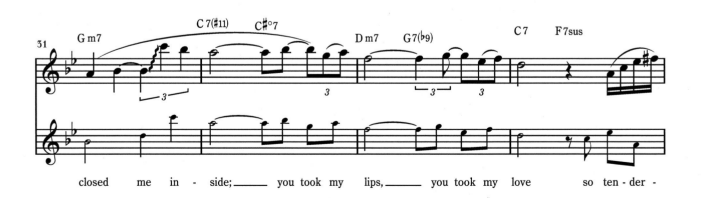

MMO 6854

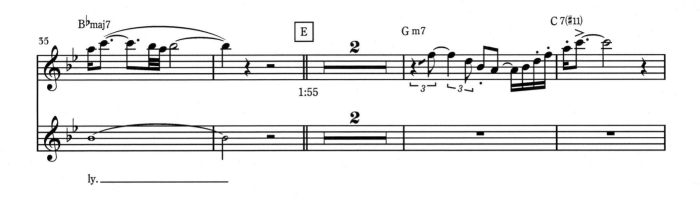

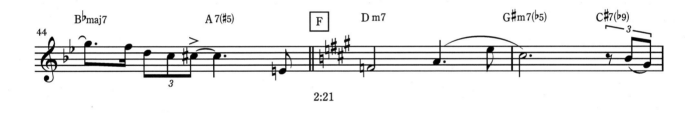

SOLO B♭ TRUMPET

Misty

Erroll Garner

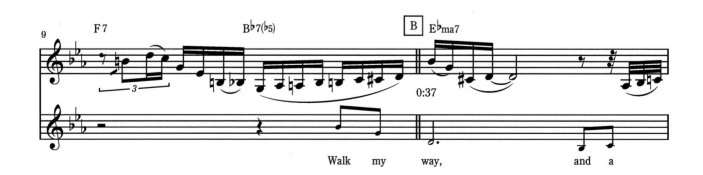

thou - sand vi - o - lins be - gin to play, or it might be the sound of your hel - lo. That

mu - sic I hear,___ I get mis - ty the mo - ment you're near.

You can say that you're lead - ing me on but it's just what I

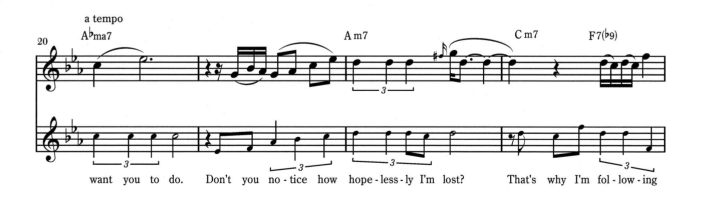

want you to do. Don't you no - tice how hope - less - ly I'm lost? That's why I'm fol - low - ing

you.   On my own,   would I

wan - der   through this won - der - land   a - lone,   nev - er know - ing my

right foot from my left,   my hat ___ from my glove?   I'm too mis - ty, and too much in

love.

SOLO B♭ TRUMPET

Hey There

Richard Adler and Jerry Ross

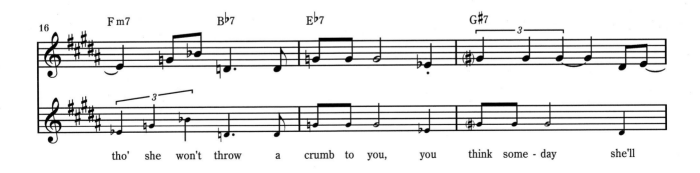

MMO 6854

20

come to you;_____ Bet-ter for - get her,_____ her with her nose in the

air, she has you danc - ing on a string, break it and she won't

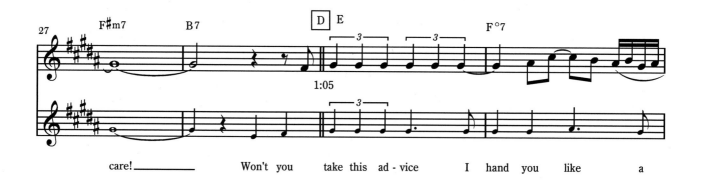

care!_____ Won't you take this ad - vice I hand you like a

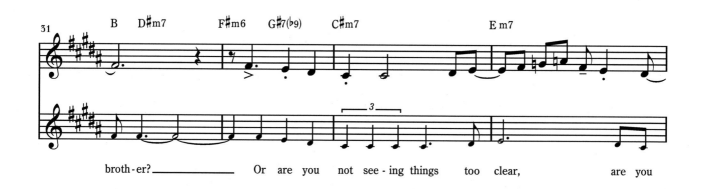

broth-er?_____ Or are you not see - ing things too clear, are you

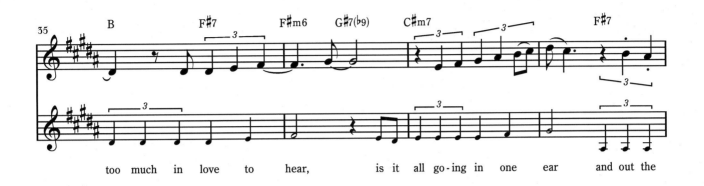

too much in love to hear, is it all go-ing in one ear and out the

oth - er?

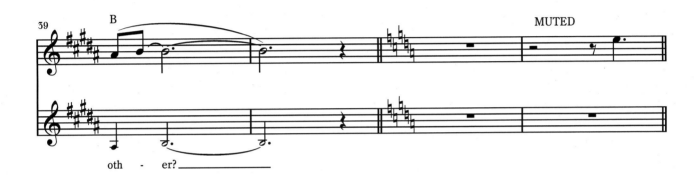

1:38

1:56

22

SOLO B♭ TRUMPET

Prisoner of Love

Leo Robin, Clarence Gaskill
and Russ Columbo

MMO 6854

24

fate now; I can't es - cape, for it's too late now,

I'm just a pris' - ner of love. What's the good of my car - ing, if

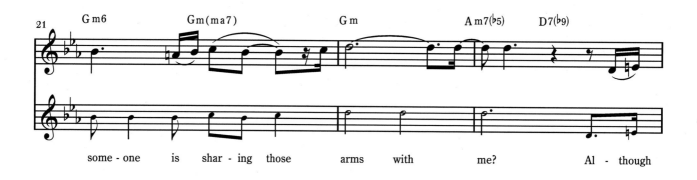

some - one is shar - ing those arms with me? Al - though

she has an - oth - er, I can't have an - oth - er for I'm not free.

MMO 6854

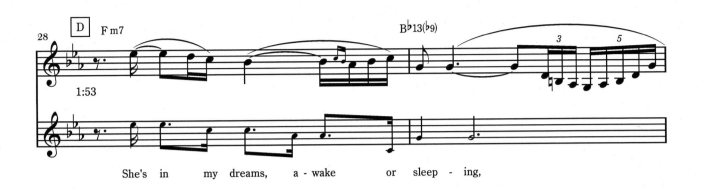

She's in my dreams, a-wake or sleep-ing,

up-on my knees to her I'm creep-ing;

my ver-y life is in her keep-ing, I'm just a pris'-ner of

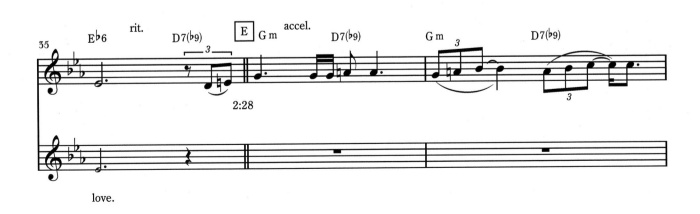

love.

26

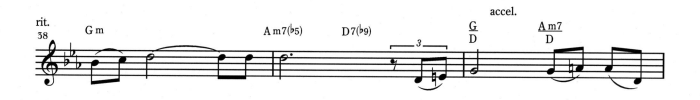

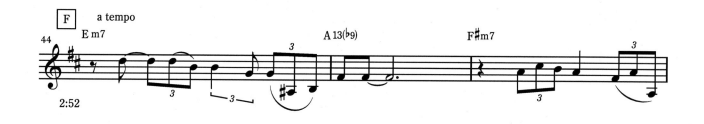

MMO 6854

SOLO B♭ TRUMPET

Love Dance

Ivan Lins, Gilson Peranzzetta,
Paul Williams and Vitor Martins

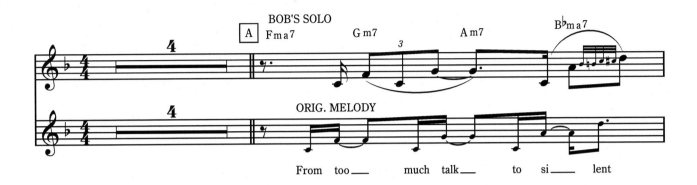

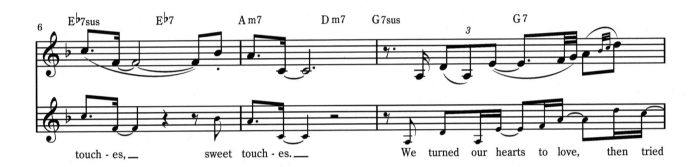

MMO 6854

28

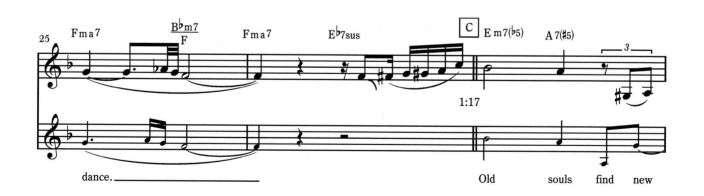

MMO 6854

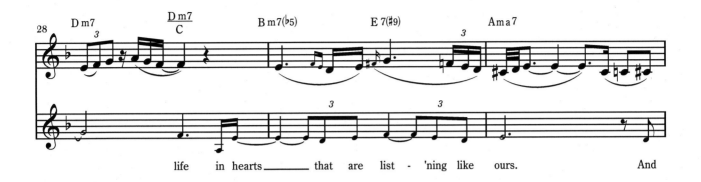

life in hearts_____ that are list - 'ning like ours.   And

old   dreams find young_____ wings   in si - - - lence,   in

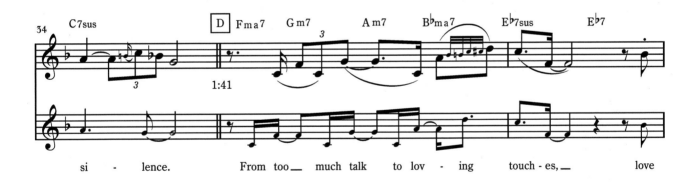

si - lence.   From too__ much talk to lov - ing touch - es,__   love

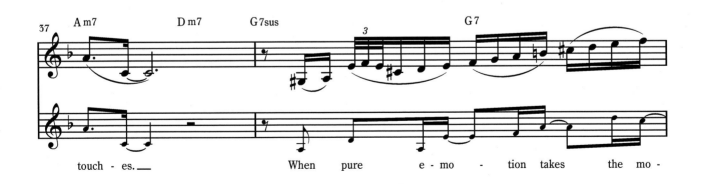

touch - es.__   When   pure   e - mo - tion takes   the mo -

30

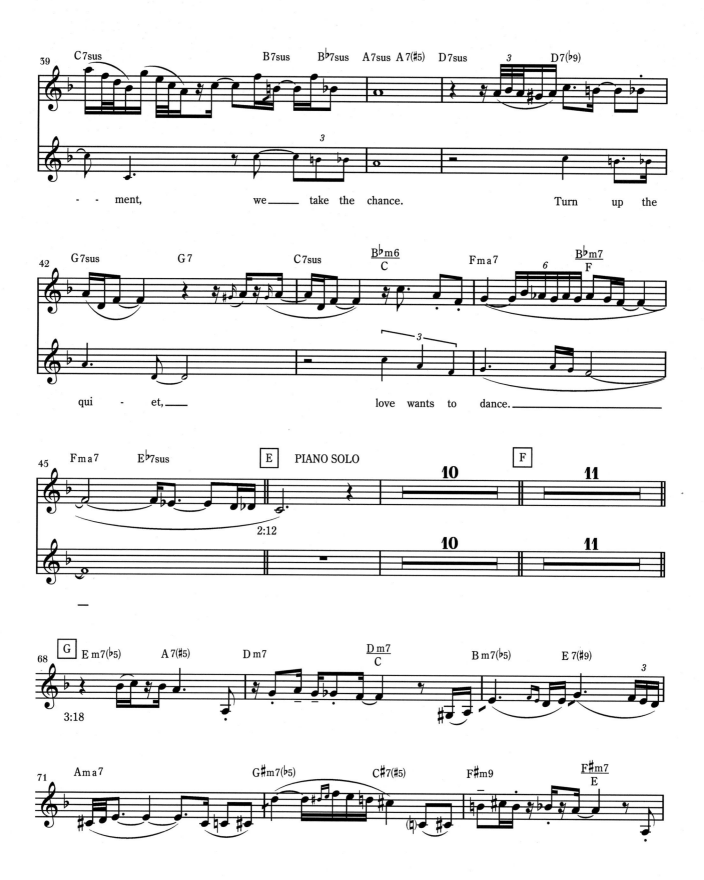

32

SOLO B♭ TRUMPET

Here's To Life

Artie Butler and Phyllis Molinary

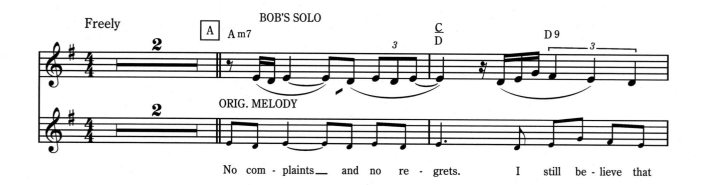

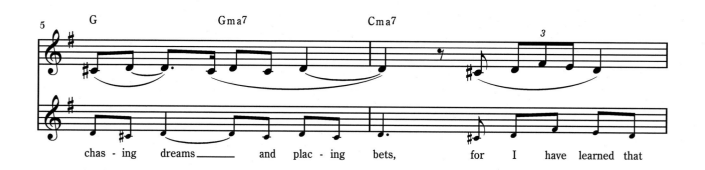

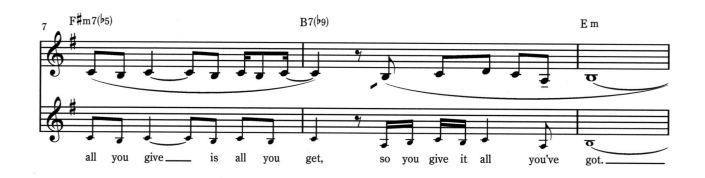

MMO 6854

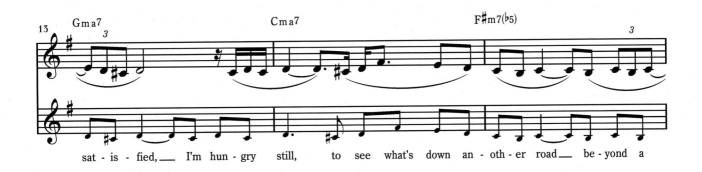

sat - is - fied,____ I'm hun - gry still, to see what's down an - oth - er road__ be - yond a

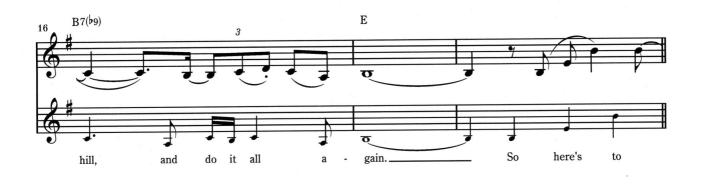

hill, and do it all a - gain.____ So here's to

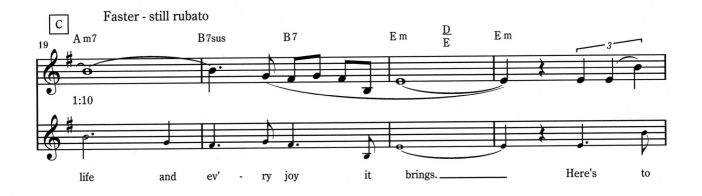

life and ev' - ry joy it brings._____ Here's to

life, to dream - ers____ and their dreams.____

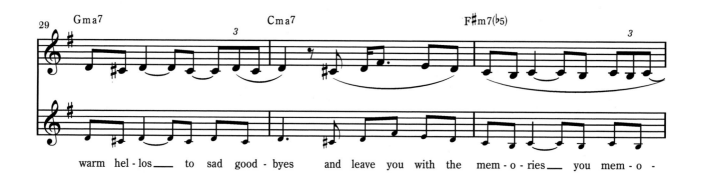

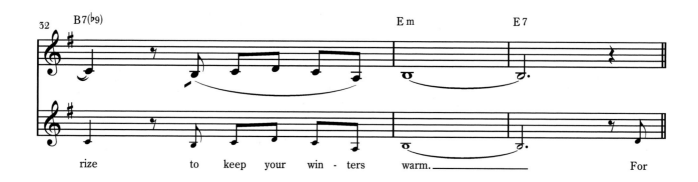

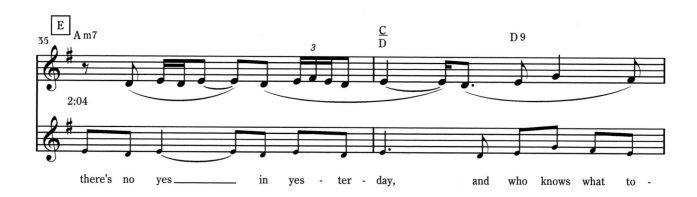

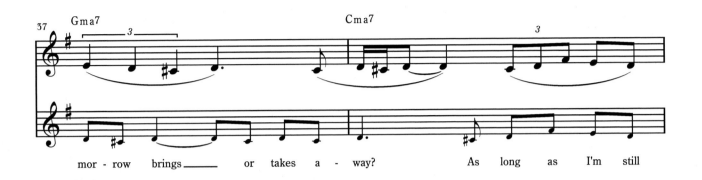

mor - row brings _____ or takes a - way? As long as I'm still

in the game, I'm gon - na play, for laughs, for life, for love. _____ So here's to

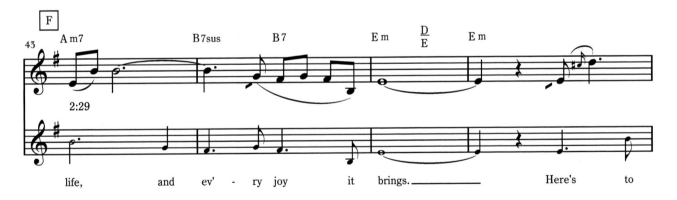

life, and ev' - ry joy it brings. _____ Here's to

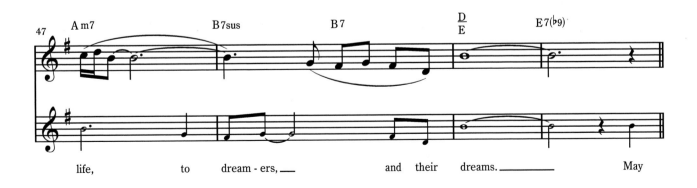

life, to dream - ers, ___ and their dreams. _____ May

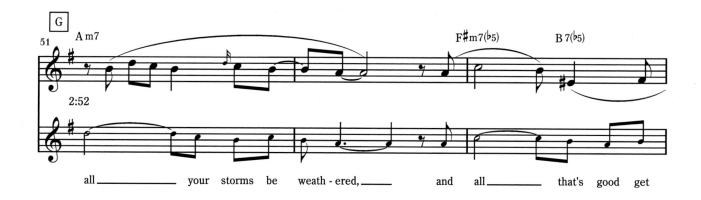

all _____ your storms be weath - ered, _____ and all _____ that's good get

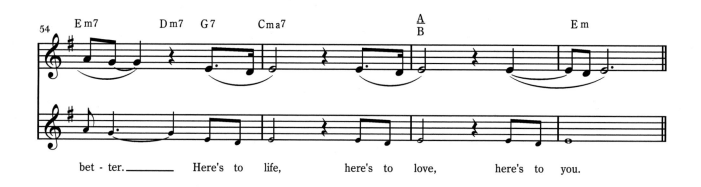

bet - ter. _____ Here's to life, here's to love, here's to you.

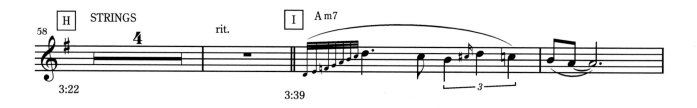

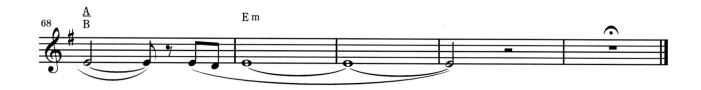

Transcription and layout by Joel Mott

Music Minus One
50 Executive Boulevard • Elmsford, New York 10523-1325
914-592-1188 • e-mail: info@musicminusone.com
www.musicminusone.com

MMO 6854

ISBN 978-1-941566-11-4